THE REAL ISSUES OF THE CANVASS;

OR,

THE NEED OF NEW MEN AND NEW MEASURES.

AN ADDRESS

BY

PARKE GODWIN.

(DELIVERED AT THE COOPER UNION, NEW YORK, OCTOBER 11TH, 1876.)

DOC. No. 17.

Read this and hand it to your neighbor. Should you need more, address, stating quantity and No. of Document desired,

NATIONAL DEMOCRATIC COMMITTEE,
Box 3637, N. Y.

THE REAL ISSUES OF THE CANVASS.

Fellow Citizens and Friends :

The Civil War, and the Constitutional Amendments it rendered necessary, closed a great era in our politics--that which grew out of the existence of slavery. The distinction of that era will be, that it determined the perpetuity of the Union ; it emancipated and enfranchised the slaves, and it ordained that the debts incurred in the prosecution of these ends should be for ever sacred, while the debts incurred in resisting them should be for ever invalid.

This great consummation having been accepted and approved by all parties, the questions it involved are taken out of the list of party questions, and are become landmarks of history. Whether wisely or unwisely settled, they *are* settled, and the nation passes on to other issues. There would be no such thing as progress in politics, if we did not admit what certain English statesmen used to call Finality. If, when a question has been fully debated and decided by the people, it can not be dismissed, our discussions would run, like mill-horses, a sterile and wearisome round, leadlng in the end to mere idiotic iteration and babble.

Thus to our war questions, other questions have succeeded which may have originated in the war, but which no longer pertain to the war. That violent commotion was stopped eleven years since ; the structural dislocations it produced are re-adjusted ; and our principal concern now is not with its causes or its management, but with its consequences.

The war left us enormous national debts, oppressive taxations, an inconvertible currency, a lax and demoralized civil service, and a vast impoverished population, whose social system was revolutionized from top to bottom. From all these sources, if ill-managed, a deluge of evils threatened us ; and the main problem of statesmanship, from that time forth the chief business of practical politics, was, by diminishing unnecessary pressures, and strengthening the requisite supports, to divert the menacing tides, through easy and natural channels, into the open fields, where they would freshen and invigorate, and not destroy.

I.—The Duty Devolved on the Party in Power.

The party in possession of the government, at the close of the war epoch, was charged with the conduct of this transition from a state of unsettled, and more or less convulsive action, to a state of regularity and order. It was obviously a work for intelligent and cautious statesmanship, and which required for its efficient execution a clear, consistent and definite policy. The finances of a nation, embracing debt, revenue, taxation and expenditure,—the currency of a nation, on which the stability and success of all its stupendous interchanges of credit and commerce depend,—the methods of the civil service, whether they shall further, or obstruct, thwart and corrupt the general interests, the harmony of localities and classes, the very basis of prosperous intercourse and social order;—these are the weightiest subjects of public concern, and the management of them, well or ill, is the real test of competency, whether in men or parties.

Now, the dominant party, which was entrusted with these important affairs,—has it recognized and discharged the responsibility? Has it seized the real objective point of the position, or only misconceived it? Has it met and overcome the actual difficulties, or has it failed to discern them, and evaded and trifled with them? That is the question to be determined by the present canvass; it is the leading, if not the sole issue; and it is to be determined, not by appeals to outworn passions, but by the evidences of reason and the facts.

Some of these evidences I propose to lay before you here; and if, in doing so, I shall trespass upon your patience, let the profound importance of the discussion be my excuse.

II.—The Republican Party has had no Policy.

Now, my first remark is, that the Republican Party has had no policy from the beginning. This was not entirely its own fault, for it was originally a war party, and war parties, from their very nature are apt to be heterogeneous in composition, and incoherent in aim and impulse. It was formed by an amalgamation of several pre-existing parties, on the spur of the moment, and to meet the conditions of an exceptional crisis. Outside the immediate issues of that crisis, its political convictions were diverse and inconsistent, according to the previous affinities of its members. This inherent vice, this incongruity of constitution, it has never been able to overcome. It has been drawn hither and thither by discrepant and irreconcilable tendencies. It has had no crystallizing idea, no dominant or organizing purpose out of which the necessary practical measures could be evolved, and consequently, no decisive or controlling policy.

Unfortunately, at the same time, it put forward no man to amend or to compensate the defects of its make up. Webster said of Hamilton, at the close of the Revolution, that "he smote the rock of the national resources, and abundant streams of revenue gushed forth ; he touched the dead corpse of public credit, and it sprang upon its feet." But, at the close of our much greater revolution, no Hamilton appeared—no leading mind capable of moulding events, or of inspiring a vast body of men with its own thought, and so creating an epoch. The Republicans, indeed, were so blind, so little sagacious, so eager for an immediate ascendancy at the expense of future mastery, that, at a time when peculiarly, as the poet sings—

> "The soldier's sword
> Should sink its point before the statist's pen,
> And the calm head replace the violent hand.——"

it selected for its leader one who was utterly ignorant of civic duties, and utterly unskilled in civic methods. He was chosen because he was a soldier, and not because he was a statesman; and the party, when it most required the aid of high political insight and ability, got no aid in that quarter, but rather increased embarrassments and difficulties.

Thus, without definite political plans, and without a competent head, the Republican party, as I shall show, has been a party of mere promises, without performance, of fluctuating councils and impotent action,—of expedients and shifts, and not of principles,—and therefore more intent on partisan than patriotic ends; leaving the good Ship of State to beat about among the rocks and shoals, as the winds shifted, or the currents sucked.

III.—Its Gross Financial Failure.

Its failure appears in every department of public affairs; but let us begin with the finances:

(1.) *Misuse of the Public Debts:* We emerged from the war with numerous and complicated debts, incurred under adverse conditions, and at high rates of interest. The first business in regard to them was to consolidate them into a single debt, at low rates,—which was practicable, and to fund the interest saved into a means of paying off the principal. Instead of this, the Republican financiers thought it a fine thing to begin paying off the debt years before it matured. Their orators and editors extolled it as a grand success and merit. It was in my opinion a grand folly. It was, moreover, a breach of law; for Congress, in 1869, had wisely enacted in the interest of honesty and resumption, that "none of the interest bearing notes should be redeemed before maturity, unless the demand notes or the legal tenders should be convertible into coin at par." Nevertheless, law or no law, the foolish practice was continued; the jubilations went on, until the convulsion of 1873 opened the eyes of more discerning men, and showed that the vacuum created in the investment market by the withdrawal of government securities had been speedily filled by railroad bonds, which enlarged the scope and aggravated the severity, if it did not produce the crisis. All the while, debts actually due from day to day, went to protest by the millions!

(2.) *Want of Economy and Extravagance.*—It is no time to pay debts already provided for, when your pockets are empty, your trade stagnant and your labor idle; but it is a time to stop waste, to check extravagance, and to get rid of parasites and bloodsuckers. Yet the administration scorned these simple dictates of prudence and good sense. Its expenditures during its last year are a hundred millions greater than in the first. In 1868–9 it spent $585,133,289; but in 1874–5, $682,000,885. No less in detail than in the aggregate has its profligacy swollen. The civil list has been increased; the costs of foreign intercourse have risen; the pensions have grown, though pensioners ought to decrease; the navy expenditures have been enormous, though we have no navy to show for it, as Admiral Porter says; the Indian bureau expands while the Indians are supposed every year to be growing fewer, and the miscellaneous outgoes, where much of the corrupt patronage comes in, leap from twenty-nine to nearly fifty millions. Read the last reports of the secretaries: not one of them proposed a single specific retrenchment of any importance. It was all give, give, give! They asked an expenditure for this year of twenty-five millions more than last year, and fifty millions more than Congress allowed. An actual burden of thirty millions was taken off our shoulders by the House of Representatives, or of $120,000 a year for each congressional district! When everybody else was at his wit's end to live, the gentlemen at Washington seem to have supposed that their offices were Big Bonanzas, with floors of silver and roofs of gold.

(3.) *Irregular and Excessive Taxation.*—Excessive expenditure, of course, means oppressive taxation; but our taxation has been more than onerous. It has been irregular, fitful, unscientific, unjust. Improvised during the war on the rule of the Irishman at Donnybrook, wherever you see a head, hit it,—wherever you find anything to tax, tax it,—it has gone on in the same careless, hap-hazard style. In other nations, both customs and excises are raised with some reference to the laws of political economy, as they are taught by science, or confirmed by long experience; but here they are imposed in a way that sets all principle at defiance. They are not laid on any definite plan, but are simply fired off at us like a French mitrailleuse which shoots a thousand missiles at a time, that explode in a thousand different directions. The tariff ought to be a short schedule of duties, selected with a view to the largest returns at the least expense, and with the slightest interference with trade; it is a formidable catalogue of exactions,—four or five thousand in kind—chosen with no purpose of revenue, but to the detriment of revenue, and solely for the benefit of a few favorites. It is a machine for extortion, which depletes the many to feed fat the few. Like the tourniquet of the elder surgeons, it arrests the circulation of one limb to accelerate that of another; but with this difference, that their instrument was applied in a state of disease to produce health, while this is used in health to promote disease. In proof, let me ask: Where are our clipper ships,—once the admiration of the world and our pride? Where our tonnage, which was once the second largest in the world, and rapidly advancing to be the largest? Where the grand ocean steamers that once carried the American flag? Gone! taxed out of existence. And yet this infernal tariff, straddling our commerce, as the Old Man of the Sea straddled Sinbad the sailor, remains! Mr. David A. Wells, an eminent statist, was engaged to infuse some degree of simplicity, order, justice and efficiency into the abominable chaos; but he was soon cashiered. The probes and correctives of science which he proposed to apply were precisely the things the system needed, but precisely the things the managers would not have. With the brilliant example of France before us, who, at the close of an invasion and a civil war, discharged an indemnity half the amount of our debt within a few years without deranging her industry, without depreciating her currency, without convulsion or paralysis, we have staggered along for eleven years, and are, in all respects, just where we began. Why the difference? The French, in their legislation, have acted on the laws of science, but we have preferred the flourish of the Donnybrook shillelah.

IV.—Circumlocution as to the Currency.

Some of this mischief is due to sheer ignorance, some of it to selfish greed; but both ignorance and greed were combined in the shameless treatment of the currency. Let me give you the whole truth of the case in a sentence which a famous Republican leader contributed to the *Tribune* not a month since. "It was in the power of the administration and "congress ten years ago," wrote Mr. Thurlow Weed, "if they "had set themselves diligently and wisely about the task, to "accomplish the resumption of specie payments, without de-"ranging or disturbing, or depressing any class or any "interest; but unhappily the statesmanship the emergency de-"manded was lacking. The administration and congress have "only been distinguished as circumlocutionists. Their efforts "thus far have been in the direction of how not to do it." That is the truth; but what perfidy, what dishonor, what disgrace it reflects upon the party which clamorously pretends to be the special friend and advocate of resumption. It was all pretence, as I shall show you by two or three memorable instances:

(1.) The acts originally authorizing the issue of legal tender notes provided for their conversion into six per cent. bonds; and if that provision had been continued, they would never have become redundant. The moment there had been an excess over the regular wants of trade they would have been invested. But within a year or two of its passage that provision of the law was repealed by the Republican congress; the broad sluices of inflation were opened, and they have ever since been kept open. Mr. Spaulding, the author of the law, has said within a week, at Buffalo, "If it had been allowed to "stand as it left my hands, if the right to fund the greenbacks "in gold bonds had not been abrogated, we should have had "specie payment in 1868"—eight years ago; "nothing under "heaven could have prevented it. The country would have "been forced into resumption in spite of itself." Why, then, was not the law allowed to stand? Because the leaders of the party were not in favor of hard money, and the party itself was never decided enough to require it of them. What better proof of this could we have than the fact that its Secretaries of the Treasury of whom we may repeat what was once said of Brougham: "they were men of brilliant incapacity, vast and "varied misinformation, and prodigious moral requirements;" have never scrupled when hard pressed, to reissue the reserve, which by law ought to have been canceled. Boutwell did it, and snapped his fingers at the law. Richardson did it, and trampled the law under his feet.

(2.) Again; in 1869, Senator Morton, who was then a hard money man (for he has boxed the compass of all opinions), proposed a bill, to accumulate gold in the treasury, and, then designate a day on which that gold should be used for the redemption of the greenbacks. The Republican Senate treated his effort with scorn; they spoke against it and voted against it; and the designation of a particular day was ridiculed and denounced as the supreme absurdity. But, they offered nothing in its place, and for five years went on debating propositions of which, as the *Evening Post* said, "it was difficult to determine whether they were the products of stolid ignorance or heartless cupidity." These debates, if such they may be called, reminded one always, of that farce of Moliére's, in which a lady having swooned, the anxious father summons in four doctors at once. They straightway fall to wrangling both as to the nature of the attack, and as to its remedies, "The case is one clearly," says the first, "of distemperature of the blood, and requires the lancet." "Not at all," interferes the second, "the humours are disordered, and we must purge." "Purge? holy heaven!" cries the third, "the patient could "not live ten minutes; it is an emetic she wants." "An emetic!"

"horror of horrors!" shouts the fourth, "'twould be instant "death, and I prescribe an anodyne." So the State doctors had each his own theory of the disease, and each his own specific. But after five years of consultation the collective faculty of the Republican College compromised, concluding that the best cure for a plethora of paper money was more money. Both the homœpathic and the allopathic schools were united in their prescription; for it was homœpathic in principle—like cures like—yet allopathic in the magnitude of the dose, which was truly heroic. In 1874 a law was passed, authorizing an inflation of $100,000.000, which, President Grant, at the last moment, and under influence that have never been explained, put to death, greatly to the annoyance of his principal supporters in Congress.

(3.) Then came one of those regurgitations of opinion, which are called tidal waves, and which threatened to change the political aspect. The Republican leaders took fright. Something must be done, they said; some tub must be thrown to the whale; and a tub was coopered up in caucus, known as the Sherman sham of January, 1875. It was nominally an act to provide for the resumption of specie payments, but really an act for the evasion of specie payments. In the face of the votes and speeches against Morton's bill, which had designated a day, its main feature was the designation of a day; but unlike that it made no provision of means. Go to! it said "on the 1st of January, 1879, let us build a tower whose top shall reach to heaven," but not a brick, nor a beam, nor a hodful of mortar was prepared. The tower was expected to go up like Solomon's temple, "without hammer or axe, or the sound of any tool." The more candid of the Republican journals, like the *Nation*, denounced the law as "a cheat." "It is a mere attempt," said the critic "of the Republican leaders to cover up their divisions," "to produce an appearance of union where no union exists, and of doing something where nothing is done." Carl Schurz in the Senate demonstrated its hollowness, and predicted its inevitable repeal; and although he voted for it, he did so in the hope that the choice of a certain day would be construed as "a pledge," and would bind the authors of it in conscience. In conscience! he did not know his colleagues. It was a pretext, a fetch, a buoy to keep them afloat, not a pledge. And the proof of their duplicity is, that as soon as the law had answered their purposes, it was abandoned. A proposition to approve it was made at Cincinnati, but instantly voted down. This "sacred pledge," this "obligation of national honor," this test and shibboleth of party orthodoxy, was ignominiously dismissed to the Limbo of Things not Wanted on Earth. Yet in the face of this ten years' prevarication, the Republican leaders have the audacity to declare "without mitigation or remorse of voice" that they alone are the friends of resumption. It must be in the sense that the hotel-keeper in Maine was in favor of the Liquor Law—*i. e.*, in favor of the law, but opposed to its execution.

(4.) The Republican party, whatever its pretensions may be, has steadily defeated resumption; for with every opportunity to bring it about, there is yet no resumption. Will any man, in the least familiar with the subject, maintain that resumption is possible without a contraction of the outstanding legal-tenders? Yet, I read in the *Tribune* of the 26th—only a few days since, an elaborate demonstration, based on a careful array of official figures, that "the currency (issued by the Government) has never been as small in volume as it was in 1867"— nine years ago, and "that it has since increased with every year." But as the Government currency is the basis of the bank-note circulation, there has been a still greater increase in that direction. In 1868,—the year of Grant's election,—the whole issue of Legal Tender notes, was $389,435,058; of Bank notes $299,-887,675, making a total of $689,322,733; whereas, in 1875,—the last year for which we have full returns, the Legal Tender notes amounted to $413,987,581; the National Bank notes to $348,216,902; or a grand total of $762,204,483. The insrease in seven years has been $72,881,750. How, in the name of logic, are we to get to resumption while the Government is moving the other way?

V.—Debasement of the Civil Service.

Incompetency and double-dealing, are exhibited in a still more striking light in respect to civil service reform. Two great and deplorable evils have been gradually grafted on our methods of administration; the one consisting in the usurpation of the executive function of appointment to office by the legislative branch, and the other, in the practice of making these appointments as a reward of mere partisan servility. The former evil was greatly aggravated by the law passed by the Republicans, which undertook to fetter the President's power of removal, and which created the senatorial conclave that has since become so dictatorial and insolent; the latter, prodigiously increased by the circumstances of the war, has grown with the strength and patronage of the government, until, as Mr. Jencks of Rhode Island, said of it in 1867,—" a more vicious system does not exist in any civilized nation on the face of the earth." It is this system, which raises men of no special qualifications to office, who do not discharge their duties at all, or discharge them badly. Mr. Curtis estimated that we lose $100,000,000 annually by maladministration. It is this system which greatly augments the number and increases the expense of the office-holders. During Grant's administration they have leaped from 54,000 to 94,000. Holding their places by an uncertain tenure, they are tempted to corrupt practices to swell their gains. The defalcations under Grant have been over $5,000,000. Owing their appointments to personal favor, not desert, they endeavour to serve those by whom they are appointed, not the public. They are Conkling's men, or Fenton's men, or Blaine's men, or Butler's, and are taken care of by their patrons. And in case of malfeasance the same influences which procured them places will endeavour to shield them from removal. No inducement to fidelity or vigilance in office, when fidelity and vigilance are not the grounds on which they are chosen or retained. On the other hand, indebted to party services for their places, they combine to hide each other's delinquencies lest their parties should suffer damage from exposure, while at times of election the entire corps is turned into a band of electioneering agents, who render political controversy, that ought to be a contest of principles, or of rival policies, a violent and bitter struggle for loaves and fishes.

Honorable and patriotic men of all parties have, since 1864, demanded the correction of these abuses. Bill after bill to suppress them has been presented and defeated in Congress. At length, in 1871, a law was enacted in compliance with an overwhelming popular sentiment, authorizing the President to prescribe rules and regulations for promoting the greater efficacy of the civil service. He instituted a commission to carry it into effect, Mr. G. W. Curtis being at the head. With what result? A loud proclamation of purposes, followed by a pompous parade, and nothing done. The active politicians including Morton, Butler, Cameron and Chandler, laughed the puny effort to scorn. Mr. Curtis, disgusted, retired from the field, amid a gentle ripple of smiles; his forlorn successor, Mr. Eaton, goes about bleating long-winded laments: and the Reform has shared the fate of those ancient victims, who were decorated with ribbons and garlands as they were led to the sacrificial altar.

How could it have been otherwise? Why, the chief of the whole concern, the President himself, set the example of treating his patronage as a personal possession, which he was at liberty to dispense, as he pleased, among his relatives and favorites. It is openly alleged that some of his principal assistants were chosen because they had contributed money to his election or made him presents. His kith and kin to the third and fourth remove were all enriched with lucrative sinecures. One or two of them obtained roving commissions that enabled them to levy tribute on contractors and applicants wherever they might be found. His boon companions were granted rich farmings of the revenues which they exploited, as the French say, as they would have used a plantation on lease. Is it strange that subordinates caught the infection, or that takers of toll stood in the vestibules of the bureaus, to sell their reputed "influence" over chiefs with whom they were, or were suspected to be in partnership?

Or, again, were the congressional managers likely to surrender a patronage on which so much of their own importance and power depended? Indeed, how were they to set up as reformers who themselves needed to be reformed? Some of them took salaries they had not earned: others accepted railroad shares for which they had legislated: nearly all would pocket the public stationery and penknives. Said Mr. Hoar, in his impeachment speech, "I have seen the chairman of the Committee on Military Affairs in the House, rise in his place and demand the expulsion of four of his associates for making sale of their official privilege of selecting the youth to be educated at our great military school. When the greatest railroad in the world, binding together the continent and uniting the two great seas which wash our shores, was finished, I have seen our national triumph and exultation turned to bitterness and shame by the unanimous report of three committees of Congress, two of the House and one of the Senate—that every step of that mighty enterprise had been taken in fraud. I have heard in highest places the shameless doctrine avowed by men grown old in public office," and who have grown old in office, but Republicans? "that the true way by which power should be gained in the republic is to bribe the people with the offices created for their service, and the true end for which it should be used when gained is the promotion of selfish ambition and the gratification of personal revenge."

VI.—Pervading Corruption of the Dominant Party.

Could any cleanliness come of such styes? Increased dirt and degradation rather! Four years ago already, Mr. Stanley Matthews, a high republican, declared, "Our party is rotten from rind to core." He was thinking, doubtless, of the Chorpenning and Secor swindles, which then looked monstrous, though they have since dwindled into dwarfs, amid their fouler companions. Four years ago, Mr. Sumner, one of the founders of the party, denounced the negotiations with St. Domingo as a venal and perfidious job, disguised under the name of a treaty. Four years ago, Mr. Carl Schurz described the sale of arms to France as a base and shabby trick, which dishonored us in the eyes of the civilized nations. Four years ago, Mr. Jacob D. Cox was shouldered out of the Interior Department because he would not allow the trading politicians to assess his clerks and run the office as a party machine.

(1.) *The revolt of* 1872.—In short, four years ago, the misrule and abuses of the administration had become so flagrant that sensitive, self-respecting men were compelled to abandon it. Messrs. Adams, Sumner, Trumbull, Schurz, Cox, Tipton, Greeley, and hundreds of thousands of others, combined for its overthrow, and, under the name of Independent Republicans, sought an alliance with the democratic opposition, in order to oust it from power. What was their complaint? In an address to the people they alleged:

1st. That the administration had openly trampled upon the law. 2d. That it had used its public functions for mere personal ends. 3d. That it had rewarded the givers of presents (or masked bribes) with honors and emoluments. 4th. That it had stood in the way of the investigation, and prevented the correction of abuses. 5th. That it had kept alive the resentments of the war, and instead of restoring the rights of the South had resorted to unconstitutional means for its oppression; and, 6th. That the Republican party upheld and justified these unscrupulous acts of corruption and despotism.

(2.) *Rapid and widespread demoralization.*—This was four

years ago, yet the party was then an angel of light compared with the dark and sinister form it has since assumed. It is since then that the Moiety Contract farmed the collection of certain revenues to a kennel of sleuth-hounds who harried respectable merchants as they used to harry fugitive negroes in the Southern swamps, and whose insolences, extortions and robberies became so outrageous that the House of Representatives, without a division, adopted the report of the Committee of Ways and Means, which declared that "the Secretary of the Treasury, the Assistant Secretary and the Solicitor deserved severe condemnation for the manner in which they had permitted the law to be enforced." It is since then that the federal army was sent into an independent and fully organized State to uphold the ascendancy of a band of adventurers from other States, who employed the money of the Custom House to secure spurious returns of elections, and the bayonets of our troops to overturn a government erected by the people. It is since then that Mr. William M. Evarts, Mr. W. C. Bryant, Mr. W. E. Dodge, Peter Cooper, Governor Saloman, and other good republicans, characterised the act, in a public meeting in New York, as "a revolutionary violence," as "an usurpation of the law," as "an outrage on legislative independence," and as "a teaching to persons receiving their first lessons in citizenship, that political problems are to be solved by arbitrary processes and displays of physical force." It is since then that a large number of prominent republican leaders have been convicted in public opinion of having taken gifts of stock from a great railroad corporation, on whose interests they had legislated or might be called again to legislate,—a Vice-President, among others, sinking into a remediless disgrace. It is since then that a Speaker of the House has shown, by his own letters, that he was a jobber in contracts, and the ally and correspondent of jobbers, whose favors he solicited on the gronnd of his rulings, and whose stocks he peddled among his adherents. It is since then that the holder of an embassy to an ancient and fastidious court, was rebuked by the House of Representatives for lending his name and his credit to a mining speculation which has taken its rank in history as among the most prodigious of frauds. It is since then that a vast conspiracy between the makers of whiskey and the revenue agents, which defrauded the Government of hundreds of millions of dollars and elected and controlled members of both Houses of Congress, has been traced to the higher departments, and even to the official household of the President. It is since then that the official instruments who exposed these enormous frauds have been frozen out or dismissed from their places, and the atmosphere which they vainly endeavored to cleanse is once more made unpleasant, not to rogues, but to the prosecutors of rogues. It is since then, finally, that we have witnessed the meanest display of venality known to our annals, that of a Secretary of War, who, as he confessed, shared in the proceeds of extortion wrung by griping post-traders from the poor soldiers of the frontier, and who, when he was impeached, allowed his counsel to defend him on the plea that the taking of gifts by public men was so common that it could not be considered blameworthy or corrupt.

(3.)—*A Corruption without parallel.*—I might add to this painful exhibition from the disclosures made by committees of the late Democratic House of Representatives, but I refrain. Not that I distrust the evidence, for I hold it to be substantially true, but lest it be said that I recur to partisan sources. It is, however, before you, and you can judge for yourselves. Fraud rises upon fraud, until, with Indian frauds, pension frauds, navy frauds, printing frauds, building frauds, contract frauds, post-office frauds, custom house frauds, and frauds upon the very grave-stones of our sacred dead—the air grows thick with malarious and suffocating vapors. As we read the dismal record, and Rings upon Rings, and Rings within Rings, are unfolded before us, we recall the dread vision of the great Italian poet, whose Infernal Regions were composed of successive circles of scoundrels and malefactors, each more doleful than the other, and stretching out into ever widening, ever deepening gloom.

(4.)—*These Crimes Confessed by Republicans.*—I rely, for my argument, I say, solely upon facts admitted by Republicans themselves. I rely upon the facts which induced President Woolsey to lament that "for the past ten years the "country had been growing politically worse, and that those "who had acted with the dominant party had reason to blush "with shame for its leaders." I rely upon the facts which prompted Mr. Carl Schurz, in May past, to exclaim "that never before, in our history, has the public mind been so profoundly agitated by apprehensions of danger arising from corrupt practices and combinations, and never was there more reason for them." I rely upon the facts which caused the liberal Republicans of this State, only last year, to "condemn the national administration for its illegal and oppressive acts," and "total disregard of law and public opinion." I rely upon the facts which led the Union League Club, of New York, to demand the emancipation of the party from the control of its habitual managers. I rely upon the facts that brought about the organization of numerous societies for "Reform within the Party," which, though a delusive hope, was none the less a confession of deplorable rottenness. I rely upon the facts which forced presidents of colleges, professors, clergymen, editors, and merchants—who, not politicians, represented the highest intellectual and moral worth of the commonwealth—to assemble in conference at the Fifth Avenue Hotel, and to consult as to what could be done to arrest the almost universal political decay. I rely upon the facts which impelled them to proclaim their determination not to support any presidential candidate connected with or conniving at corruption, and who was not in character and by record, capable of striking down "the enormous abuses intrenched behind established custom."

VI.—The Effort to Disguise and Evade Responsibility.

"But," say a class of meek-eyed Republicans, adopting the phrase of Moliére's mock-doctor, when some one insisted, contrary to his saying, that the heart was on the left side of the body, *nous avons changé tout cela*, we have changed all that! What you describe, they say, what all these indignant classes protest against, is Grantism—not Republicanism! Alas! the distinction, is like that of the bishop who had fallen into the vice of profane swearing, and who excused himself for the fault on the ground that he swore as a man and not as a bishop. "But when the man is damned for it," asked a bystander, "what will become of the bishop?" What will become of Republicanism, when Grantism goes below? I am not at all surprised at the desire to get rid of the connection. Nobody likes to go about with an ill-smelling companion—a dead dog, or a consumer of garlic. Nevertheless everybody ought to be held to the consequences of his acts. Party government means that parties, not persons, are the responsible instruments of power. No doubt it would be convenient to make a scapegoat of Grant, and, after putting the sins of a whole community of rascals on his shoulders, send him into the wilderness. But that vicarious ceremony would not change the real state of the facts. Grant has been the incarnation of his party.

(1.)—*Grant never Renounced, but always Approved.*—Has he ever been renounced? If so, when and where? A few bold speakers and writers, now and then, have dared to criticise his management, but they were at once excommunicated, like Sumner, Schurz, Trumbull and others. The mass of the party has clung to him. It was only a year or two since it was doubtful whether he would not be proposed for a third term. His friends say still that he would poll more Republican votes than any man named as a candidate at Cincinnati. Certainly the party, when acting as a party, has never lost an occasion for approving his management. State conventions are commonly considered the exponents of party sentiment! Well, how has it been with them? I have taken pains to consult the records for the past year, and I find that not a single one of them ventured to breathe a word of reproach.

(*a.*)—*By the State Conventions.*—From Maine to Oregon expressions of approval followed each other like a *fau de joie* of musketry. Massachusetts said, "the President is entitled to our gratitude for his independence, courage and good sense." Kentucky professed "unabated confidence in his devotion to Republican principles." Connecticut repeated its "undiminished confidence in his integrity and patriotism;" and Ohio was sure that "he is an able and judicious statesman, entitled to our gratitude." Iowa, Minnesota, Mississippi, Arkansas all avowed "a hearty approval," while far California "joined her political brethren of the Union in their cordial and earnest support of the administration." But Pennsylvania capped the climax, proclaiming "the achievements of the administration the most brilliant in our annals." Well; they are the most brilliant, but the brilliancy was that which came from putrescence!

(*b.*)—*By the National Convention.*—When the National Convention assembled at Cincinnati, only three months since, this chorus of peans again assaulted the patient heavens. All the leading men of the party were there; and was anything said, either in the speeches or resolutions, to disparage Grantism? Was it proposed, even by implication to discard its spirit and its methods? Did any one so much as hint as to the necessity or the propriety of great and searching reforms? Was reform mentioned at all? Not a word! The administration was again praised to the top of the gamut. For all that was said, Babcock was an unborn babe of innocence, and Belknap's ghost, which must have stalked among them, stalked unrebuked. It was conceded, it is true, that the public conscience was somewhat aroused, and that if malfeasance and crime should, perchance, be discovered, they ought to be punished, but as to the streams of feculence which had poured for the last ten years through all the public orifices they were as dumb as driven cattle. The cry for reform, that has been gathering strength from day to day, and from hour to hour, until it had almost swollen to the might and majesty of a tempest, beat and roared around the edifice where the collective wisdom of Republicanism was assembled but in vain; its pleading voices were drowned in the howl of the placemen over their endangered provender. What! reform in a convention, where a man fearfully shattered by his own letters, came within twenty-five votes of the Presidential nomination, while the man who had earnestly labored to put down corruption received no more than 126 out of a total of 756 votes!

(2.)—*The same Managers and the same Machinery employed.*—Grantism discarded! Look you; the most devoted henchmen of the administration—the notorious Senatorial Ring which has defended its every act—are still the leading managers! Cameron, Conkling, Morton, Logan, to whom Blaine has recently been added, are the Ajax Telemons of this campaign. Chandler, Grant's Secretary of the Interior, a weather-beaten trickster, who has come down to us from former generations, is the chosen center of the machine, and turns the crank. Every placeman, from the highest bureaucrat to the lowest tide-waiter, has joined the hunt, and "harks forward" the pack, which, according to the Republican reformers, must turn him out of his hole? Would every scoundrel from Colfax to Schenck, every suspected pilferer whom the late inquiries have branded, fling up his cap for the regeneration of a party, which, if regenerated, must forever exclude him from its embrace? Would the whole "bread and butter brigade" of office holders turn out as "Boys in Blue,"—though some of them were infants in arms, not soldiers in arms,—during the war—if they expected the besom of reform to sweep their ranks? The mere supposition is absurd. In ancient times, when a man got possessed of the devil, they cast the devil out; but now the practice is to get rid of the evil spirit by keeping him in! Is it reform to employ the very men who have debauched and debased a party to plead its cause before the people? Is it reform to go about making speeches which touch upon every other topic but reform? Read the campaign orators! Their whole talk is a war whoop! They go back sixteen years to dig up issues from the decay of the grave; they go forward indefinitely into the future to invent issues, like the "rebel claims" which are conjectural and preposterous; but existing abuses they avoid, as the proverb says, the devil does holy water. The only abuse they handle is the abuse of personal character, in which they display a prodigality of resource that might fill all Billingsgate with envy.

(3.)—*The Republican Reformers Impotent.*—There is no doubt a small but highly respectable minority of the Republicans, the "better element" it is called (though Mr. Conkling lately said they were "only theorists or critics, or professional reformers, or vainglorious pretenders to supreme wisdom"), which really desires to wash away the sins of the party, which believes in reform within the party, and has labored diligently to that end. All honor to its efforts! But thus far, I say, its members have fought a losing fight. They were twice defeated in this State; they have been defeated in every other State where they have tried it on, save one; and they were defeated in the National Convention, when they were compelled to accept a candidate who was not their choice. They took him, not because he was the man they wanted, but because they supposed he might turn out better than others whom they did not want. They achieved no triumph of principle; they simply submitted to a party stratagem. I doubt, in fact, whether the reform of a party which has fallen into bad ways because of its long possession of power be morally possible from within. History would seem to demonstrate that in all ages, or in ninety-nine cases out of a hundred, reformers are compelled to be come-outers. They must abandon the organization, which they desire to purify, if they would make their blows effective. Within it they are crushed by its force, or defeated by its cunning; and the same influences, the same temptations, which have caused its degeneracy will baffle their efforts. It will go on festering in its iniquity. It will go on deteriorating till adversity overtakes it, and shakes it out of its routine, and drives away the ill-omened birds who have fouled it with their droppings. In this view, Mr. Schurz, in 1872, contended that the Republican party was so pervaded and subjugated by the spirit of corruption that the reformation of it was not be to expected.

"A political party," he said, "which fails to recognize "abuses, as such, has lost the moral ability to correct them. "Its very ascendancy will thenceforward *stand in the way of "reform.* * * * And thus it is that the "great name, the great authority of the Republican party "is being used this very moment to uphold the most atrocious "system of government which this country ever saw. A "party which cannot live and prosper unless it be supported "by corruption; a party that cannot prosper unless it be sup- "ported by a revival of the old war feeling, and by tearing "open again the wounds from which the people of the United "States have bled so long; such a party, when it has come to "that, does not deserve to live."

VII.—Mr. Hayes is only a Makeshift.

Mr. Hayes, the new leader, whom all the factions unite in supporting, may or may not be the Hercules, destined to cleanse their Augean stable—who can tell? He is quite unknown, and the auguries are not favorable. He was not, in the first place, chosen in the way that reformers are commonly chosen, *i. e.*, because of their prominence as reformers. His name had never been, in the slightest degree, identified with the movement for the amelioration of Republican politics. All through the outbreak and revolt of the "better element" which is spoken of, he never so much as whimpered. During the whole misuse of power, which the reformers complain of, not a word of dissatisfaction, not even a lisp of criticism, escaped his lips.

(1)—*The Mode of his Selection.*—Neither inside nor outside the nominating convention was he spoken of as the representative or the ally of those who desired a change. Those who were on the outside, in a public address, had expressly excluded men of his calibre from their lists of possible choice; those on the inside had previously described and deprecated the very course of proceeding by which he was selected. Mr. Curtis, a leader of the latter sort, had (in *Harper's Weekly*), some weeks before the convention, directed attention to the peculiar mode in which the Pennsylvania delegation was constituted; it was pledged to vote as a unit for Hartranft, who had no chance, and that meant, he said, that they should keep Hartranft as a dummy in the foreground, until the time should arrive for springing another, but no less serviceable name. Now the very procedure which Mr. Curtis predicted and feared was the procedure which the delegation followed. Hartranft was voted for till the opportune moment came, when he was thrust into the bag, and Mr. Hayes was pulled out of it. At once all the trading members rushed to the rescue. They all gave cry, as young dogs at fault when they hear the yelp of some older hound. Strange to say, the reformers joined in, and with Cameron on the lead,—Cameron, a name identified with the dirtiest tricks of politics in the dirtiest of the gangs—yelped as loudly as the others. It may be possible, as a wit has said, that by setting a fresh hen on a nest of rotten eggs, you are going to hatch out a fine brood of chickens, but that is not the way of nature.

(2.) *Mr. Hayes's Serviceable Qualities.*—Mr. Hayes is only a new hen; the nest is the same, and the eggs are the same. I shall, however, say nothing against Mr. Hayes, for the reason that some one gave for not fighting a duel with the lank John Randolph—there was not enough of him to shoot. I have just read his biography, put forth by admiring friends, and I find it a labored canonization of the merest mediocrity. He had the merit some years ago, common to about five hundred thousand of our fellow citizens, of serving honorably in the war; but he served with no particular distinction. He was four years in Congress, where his name was heard only when the clerk called the roll. No measure of his devising is now remembered; not a speech even remains; not so much as a report on any subject, save a resolution which he got in from the most insignificant of committees, that on the Library. It was a proposal to give away a considerable number of books to the members themselves, which Elihu Washburne snubbed by the remark that if they wanted the property of the people they ought to pay for it, and not endeavor to pocket it by a sneaking appropriation! Hayes simply voted with his party, which means that he voted for all the gigantic subsidies to the Pacific Railroads, for many bad jobs, and for the several measures which looked to an inflation of the currency. Mr. Hayes has also been a Governor of Ohio for several years; it is a clerical office, calling for the exercise of no marked ability, but, such as it is, his management of it does not seem to have been resplendent. The *Boston Daily Advertiser*, a Republican sheet, describing his career, said: "He has been "Governor for two terms, but there never was any danger that "he would institute any reform to hurt. He is a man of fair "ability, good-natured, correct in his personal habits, honest,

" sound in the Republican faith, but of no force or independ-" ence." That, I suspect, is a correct description ; it is what those who know him in his own State have written me, and it was the opinion of Mr. Carl Schurz expressed to me not long ago. Mr. Hayes never has been a leader in the true sense of the term. He always has been a follower, and very likely always will be.

(3.) *Poor Material for a Reformer.*—Now, you will confess that this is poor timber for a reforming Hercules. Certainly, it is not what the Fifth avenue conference demanded, when, in terms which they again and again emphasized, they asked for a candidate who should be something more than " an availability ;" a candidate who was not to be trusted merely " on the " strength of private recommendations," or upon " supposed virtue and rumored ability." They demanded " a candidate " who might be depended upon to possess the moral courage " and sturdy resolution to grapple with abuses that have ac-" quired the strength of established custom." These very words were written and uttered, as I know, to prevent the candidacy which some of their writers and utterers now profess to regard as satisfactory. Politics, like time, has its whirligigs, and no gyratory display will, in the end, prove more remarkable than that which loudly clamored for a reform, and quietly accepted a succession.

VI.—The Attitude of the Democratic Reformers.

Thus far you have seen the shortcomings, the blunders, the deceits and the rascalities of the ruling party ; you have seen the depth and extent of its official degradation as depicted by its own members ; but you will ask whether the Democratic reformers are likely to do any better ? That is a pertinent and a decisive question, and I am going to answer it frankly. But before answering it, permit me to make two preliminary observations. The first is, that if there is to be any change at all in the political situation, it must be through the only organized political force capable of the task ; that is the Democratic party. The Republican party, will not, as we assume, cleanse itself ; a third party is impracticable, and therefore, unless you are willing to grant an eternal lease, an eternal monopoly, to the party in possession, you must make use of the only remaining weapon of resistance. In the second place, that part of the republican party which calls itself

Liberal cannot object to a co-operation with the Democratic party. It cannot, because it is estopped by its own example. In 1872 its journals, with the *Tribune* at their head, teemed with appeals to the people to take that party to their embraces, Its most distinguished leader, Mr. Greeley, traversed the land commending it, in speeches of remarkable power, to general confidence. Mr. Carl Schurz went so far as to say that its willingness to ally itself with the Independents, in spite of its dislike for Mr. Greeley, atoned for all its past misconduct, and evinced a nobleness of self-surrender that was itself a pledge of its future virtue. In a word, the liberal revolters besought it alliance, and were willing and eager to trust it with all the responsibilities of power. Were these gentlemen sincere then? what was the ground of their faith? Are they sincere now? what is the ground of their distrust? There was then, or there is now, some prevarication, and I leave them to choose the horn of the dilemma on which they wish to be impaled. Certainly, the Democratic party has not degenerated in the interval; but, on the contrary, as I am about to show, it has greatly improved.

(I.) *The Democratic Declaration of Principles.*—Its remarkable declaration of principles, made at St. Louis—the most penetrating, clear and comprehensive creed yet uttered by any of our political parties—shows that it has a thorough conception of the existing evils, and of the remedies by which they are to be reached. Accepting in unreserved and emphatic terms the constitutional and social changes wrought by the war, it proposes as the basis of all future legislation, both State and national, the perfect equality of citizens before the law. It denounces as an invasion of this fundamental tenet those paternal and fostering theories of the functions of government, which have always been the fruitful sources of injustice and tyranny. In this condemnation it includes that spirit of petty interference with the concerns of society, which ultimates in sumptuary and inquisitorial legislation, whose peculiar sphere is the kneading trough and the bed-chamber. In a word, it returns to those grand principles of human rights and human freedom which identify Democracy with Christianity, and, on the strength of these, it demands a searching, smiting, unsparing reformation of specified abuses,—in finance, in taxation, in currency, and the civil service. Every word is full of meaning, and breathes alone of amelioration and progress.

It seems to me impossible for any ear to mistake their ring of sound and sonorous metal. The great aims on which we reformers of old date have fixed our eyes—decentralization, hard money, free trade, impartial legislation, are here made the rallying cry of a vast and powerful body of men, and for us to reject the overture would be as foolish as it would be for the General of a forlorn hope to turn away a mighty reinforcement, and go over to the foe on the very eve of victory.

(2.)—*Sincerity of its Purposes.*—It will be said, I am aware, that the Democrats are not sincere in this avowal of their faith; and some of them are not; for parties, like drag nets, catch up many queer fish; but I find it impossible to believe that a body embracing one-half the people of the United States, at least, is insincere. As for the authors of that platform, I know them to be terribly in earnest. Of the Democratic Party itself, it should be remembered, that separated for years from official responsibility, it has been an inchoate and desultory opposition rather than a compact organization. It has suffered the fate of most oppositions; nearly all the unswept rubbish of discontent has been shot into its bosom; nearly all the extravagance and vagary that accredited authorities must repulse has assumed its name, while its own impatience of misrule has fermented into sour eructations, or caused it to fling out before and behind in a wild way that has often damaged itself more than its enemy. It has, however, none the less profited by its own follies and mistakes, and I look upon its remarkable action at St. Louis as a most hopeful recovery from its past errors. I see its earlier and better traditions—forgotten for a time in the giddy whirl of a tempest,—there revived; I recognize there its old instinct of justice, its old popular sympathy, its old aspiration for freedom and progress, and I believe that now—recruited by many of the soundest heads and noblest hearts of the other camp, by Adamses, Trumbulls, Palmers, Curtins, Blairs, Hoadleys, Welleses and Bartletts, who have been driven forth by its corruptions—and, infused with the fresh, ardent, uncontaminated blood of the young men, such as I have before me—it is destined to resume the vigor and splendor of its prime.

(3.)—*The Democratic Candidate.*—Its choice of a leader reinforces this faith and confirms this confidence. Mr. Tilden is, of all men living, one of the best fitted to the position and the times. We of this city, at least, know who and what he is.

He has gone in and out before us for forty years, and our eyes are our witnesses. He has gone in and out before us, as the respected private citizen, as the eminent lawyer, as the adroit but upright politician, as the reformer whose brows are gashed with tokens of old wars, yet wreathed with the laurels of as many victories, and as the experienced statesman, whose work, as far back as 1846, had been incorporated into our constitution and our history.

(*a.*)—*Partisan misrepresentations.*—Yet, singular to say, a rancorous partisan press, which combines the manners of the bravo with those of the fishwife, has declared that we are mistaken in these experiences of forty years, and that Mr. Tilden is not only not what he pretends to be, or what we believe him to be but something far different. It has found as many bad names for him as Coleridge found of bad smells in Cologne. He is a drunkard, a liar, a cheat a counterfeiter, a perjurer and a swindler,—whose pretensions as a reformer are put on only to hide his companionship with thieves; and whose fortune has been won, not by the honorable use of a rare and exceptional talent, but in low intrigue and fraudulent devices. The dirty hounds! If what they yelp at his heels were true he would still be purer than many in power at Washington, but, none the less, he ought to be in Sing Sing, not, the Governor of the largest state of the Union.

But, unhappily for their authors, these are bald, atrocious, unpardonable falsehoods; the spawn of reckless brains and malignant hearts. I sometimes shudder at the dark fog-bank of calumny which an electioneering heat engenders; and yet I cannot think that the pupil and friend of Silas Wright, Michael Hoffman and Azariah Flagg,—New York's traditional synonymns for public probity,—that the friend and companion of Cutting, Kent, Sedgwick, Bryant, O'Conor and Robinson; that the leader whom forty thousand Democrats of this city followed in his relentless charge upon the banditti of the City Hall, whom the people of the State, for that service, chose their Governor by a majority of fifty-four thousand over the once amiable but now gory-minded General Dix; whom his very opponents lately delighted to praise; I say I have greatly mistaken the character of the American people if such a man with such a career, is to be injured by whole simooms of slander, however foul or violent.

(*b.*)—*Confessions of his opponents.*—The very fabricators of these libels were Mr. Tilden's eulogists not two years since. He is, said the *Times*, "a high-toned Democrat," "a man of unsullied honor, public and private," "a gallant, conscientious, efficient foe to corruption;" "of an honesty beyond all question," and "deserving the greatest credit for the good work he has done and the evil work he has frustrated." Need I add the testimony of the *Tribune*, the *Evening Post*, the *Nation*, and *Harper's Weekly?* Take one only—the last. You all know and admire my accomplished friend, Mr. G. W. Curtis—too much of a partisan, perhaps, but a gentleman and a scholar, What said he hardly a year ago? "In opposing his election " (for Governor) we were careful never to question his ability, " or his integrity. When he took hold of the Reform movement " against Tweed, he did so with a vigor, a tenacity and a SUCCESS " *that every good citizen could most sincerely commend.* Tilden is " a man of great political experience and sagacity. He knew " that in his efforts he had necessarily alarmed the immense " venal element of his party, and that he must count upon " its constant and relentless hostility. No man knew better " than he the power, the secresy, the resources and the methods " of that conspiracy for plunder and fraud known as the Ring. " Happily his instincts and his experience assured him that " the people are not corrupt, and that a bold, radical and " thoroughly intelligent assault upon entrenched and enormous " abuses is sure of public sympathy and support." "In the " course that Governor Tilden has taken in defying, exposing " and routing the Canal Ring he will be supported by all " honest citizens."

(c.)—*The very man for the Crisis—then?*—Why then, my excellent and eloquent friend, should he not be supported by all honest citizens in the course that he proposes to take "for defying, exposing and routing" the much larger and more damaging rings that encircle and fetter every limb of the Federal administration? He has the "instinct" you allege; he has "the ability"; he has "the integrity"; he has "the courage"; he has "the experience"; he has every quality for a "bold, radical and intelligent assault upon entrenched abuses," and is he not then the very man? With his exceptional knowledge of finance and kindred subjects of political economy; with his rare talent for business, which is universally conceded by capitalists and business men; and with his definite convictions as to the problems which perplex our statesmanship; with all these added to the qualities which Mr. Curtis ascribes to him, the answer leaps to the eyes, the "Hour and the Man" have met.

(3.)—*Consequences of Mr. Tilden's Success.*—Yes; let Governor Tilden be elected to the Chief Magistracy, and I should look with as much confidence, as it is possible to contemplate events that are future, to these grand and desirable results; I should expect a rigid retrenchment of the public expenditures and new economies introduced into every branch of public business; I should expect the introduction of that systematic method of taxation that science and experience alike approve; I should expect a regeneration of the civil service, according to the luminous view of the Letter of Acceptance, which would comprise (*a*) the elevation of the standard of appointment; (*b*) conscientious fidelity in the exercise of the power to remove; (*c*) the abolition of unnecessary and parasitic functions; (*d*) and the organization of a system, in which competence, integrity and diligence—not as now, mercenary, personal and partisan services—should be the sole test of eligibility. I should expect the restoration of our finances, including the currency, by a series of clear-sighted, wisely-devised, nicely graduated measures, that would bring us to a normal condition, without convulsion or injury to trade, and yet with an assurance of movement to which every interest might easily be adapted and conformed; and, finally, I should expect a conciliation of the entire South by a firm protection of the rights of all, which, while it would take away the heavy arm of interference, would open the channels through which our stagnant Northern capital would flow in fertilizing streams over its parched and barren deserts, and the hands now raised against each other in menace would be too busy for any work but that of peaceful, useful labor.

VI.—The Ex-Confederate Spectre.

The South! aye, that is it! "Prythee! see there! look! behold!" the Ex-Confederates! I look, and see large squads of placemen, raising a cry of alarm to divert the gaze of the public from their own peculations and frauds. Behind them I see a crowd of credulous and long-eared followers, who people the vacancy with phantoms that exist only in their own fears. As I approach more nearly, the embodied Awe, the incarnate Dread, the mysterious Gorgon, resolves into a scooped pumpkin with a candle in it, shining through the mist. What, in the name of all the stuffed and ragged scarecrows that ever fluttered, are these Ex-Confederates going to do? What can they do? "Re-enslave the freedmen!" stammers one; yes I answer, when the instinct of justice is stifled in every American heart, and the demon of despotism sits triumphant on the ruins of our most cherished institutions. "Recognize the rebel debt," whispers another; yes, when it is carried through by two-thirds of each House of Congress and three-fourths of all the States, which will be when Bismarck is cannonized by the College of Cardinals, or Sitting Bull appointed to the place of General Sherman. "Pile up claims for losses incurred in the Rebellion,' mutters a third; yes; and the higher they are piled the more sure they are to topple, and surest of all under the Democratic policy of economy and retrenchment. Pshaw! these are the shallow devices of electioneering zeal, and no more worthy of heed than the cry of the fellow who halloed fire in the midst of the deluge.

(1.)—*A Creation of Guilty Consciences.*—I, however, do not wonder that the South, like Banquo's ghost, should fill the Republican leaders with alarm. When she rises before them—pale, dishevelled and broken—their guilty consciences, if they have any, must sting and tremble. Of all the misdeeds of partisan greed and malignity, there is none more foul and atrocious than that which has tried to enforce a foreign and corrupt despotism upon the Southern people. For a parallel to it we must look to the doings of Austria in Italy, or of Great Britain, aforetime, in Ireland The South came out of the war prostrate and benumbed; her capital was gone; her labor annihilated; her social system uprooted and destroyed. She had fought for a false idea—fought bravely, fought desperately—frantically and cruelly sometimes; but she had fought in vain. Her cause was lost—and lost forever. It was lost, not as a fact merely, but as an illusion. Every discerning mind saw that for her nothing was left but to gather up the wreck, restore the waste places, and to re-knit the broken ties. A few lingering rancors, born of the contest, flickered here and there, impotent as they were foolish, but the deeper antagonisms were all crushed. For us, as for them, the single duty of the hour, imposed by a regard to the common prosperity, as well as by a sentiment of kindliness, was, in the fine language of Governor Andrew, "to prosecute peace as vigorously as we had prosecuted war." So that, where once all day "the noise of battle rolled," should be heard again the melodies of joy and concord, ringing like a chorus of birds when the black storm clouds are past.

The South was, peculiarly, repentant and placable. General Grant himself, in a report made soon after the war, bore evidence of the universal desire of the people for the resumption of friendly relations. General Dix, Henry J. Raymond, and a hundred other Republicans, assembled at Philadelphia to promote a fraternal feeling, said: "The concurrent testimony of "those best acquainted with the condition of society and the "state of public sentiment in the South, establishes the fact "that the great mass of the Southern people accept, with as "full and sincere submission as do the people of the other "States, the re-established supremacy of the national authority, "and are prepared in the most loyal spirit and with a zeal "quickened alike by their interest and pride, to co-operate "with other States in whatever may be necessary to defend "the rights, maintain the issues, and promote the welfare of "the common country."

Such the promises of the dawn after a dark and stormy night; full of hope and cheer and brightness; but ere long base clouds and rack and rotten smoke thickened the air and stained the skies. Whence the change? You know its history; I shall not repeat it; Professor Sumner, in his able and impressive letter, has said all that needs to be said; there stands the salient facts! You know how miscreant adventurers—the scum and offscouring of the North—sowed the seeds of division among the races; you know how successive flights of these birds of prey, "with appetites continually renewing for food continually wanting," consumed the little substance which war had spared; and you know that once in power they turned every agency of government into a means of robbery and spoliation. The unhappy States they sequestered became like provinces of the Indian Empire, in the time of a Hastings or a Clive, saving that this record of vulgar rapacity was unbroken by one mark of high ability or one act of generous forbearance. What is worse, this ascendency of conspiring scoundrels, which insulted and exiled the whites, "the natural leaders of society," which debauched and misled the blacks, and which for ten years has kept open a seething cauldron of turbulence, blood and anarchy, was sustained by the Federal Government with our money and our arms. Oh! the cruelty of it; oh! the shame of it. Once it was our boast that a handful of Americans, chance thrown upon a desert coast, or meeting by accident in a wilderness, would improvise a fabric of stable and orderly government; but here we have a powerful party, with every means and appliance at its control, utterly impotent to maintain a decent order in societies long inured to freedom and self-management; and proclaiming, at the end of ten years of trial, through the mouth of its Boutwell, that it sees no remedy but in military force, or in remanding those States to the condition of Territories; while its President, on the hundredth anniversary of our popular institutions, tells the assembled world that free elections are possible, in half of the Union, only under a menace of bayonets.

(2.)—*The South not to be Feared.*—Now, I have no fears of the South; on the contrary, I have every reasonable confidence in the South. Is there, indeed, any longer a South in any distinctive sense? The only cause of sectional division that ever existed—slavery—is gone, and the shadow of it hardly remains. We are united now, in interest, in feeling, in nationality, and in civilization, as we were never before united. We are all Americans, without regard to locality; we are all citizens, without regard to condition; and if the States once disaffected are returned to that freedom of self rule which obtains in the other States, their unhappy color divisions which have been factitiously excited and fostered will melt into the simple political divisions of our own peaceful communities. They will engage in the same discussions, follow the banners of the same parties; and whites and blacks, sharing in the same rights and interests, will go marching forward, side by side, to the same great national ends. Or, if there should be a difference, it would be perhaps in this—their superior warmth of devotion to the cause of equal laws and impartial legislation. They have felt with peculiar anguish—they have borne with peculiat patience—the miseries of a long misrule; and will they not value with peculiar affection the needs of peace, and the blessings of upright government? Where the blood of Washington, Jefferson, Madison and Marshall still circulates—where the intellects of Lowndes, Gaston and Pettigru are still revered, the civic virtues, which are the salvation and the ornament of States, can not wholly be extinguished.

Away, then, with that culture of distrust and hatred, which, like a malarious swamp, can nourish no seeds of good, can diffuse only the germs of blight and death! The late Mr. Sumner, whose devotion to his cause was like the zeal of a lover was yet unwilling that trophies of victory won by citizen over citizen should be preserved among the national archives; and shall we, less magnanimous than that great soul, insist, like pagan conquerors, upon dragging our victims, lashed to the wheels of our triumphal chariots, amid the jeers of a rabble? Or, baser still, in the dark fanaticism of the middle ages, turn their skins into drums whereon to beat the tattoo of hellish partisan rallies? Are we Christians? Are we patriots? Are we men? Or, do the vestiges of the brute and the savage, from which, according to modern theories, we are evolved, still survive in our veins?

(4.)—*A Call for Centennial Concord and Peace.*—No; our Democratic civilization, illustrated by many a heroic deed, has none more noble than the closing scenes of the war, when on the one side, a vast and victorious army, dispersed to its peaceful avocations, like mists of night melting in the sunrise; and, on the other side, a gallant, but stricken foe, resumed their allegiance to a polity which brought with it the most tremendous social and political change ever wrought in any human society. The sublimity, the magnificence, the glory of that great conclusion can never be lessened; but as the French proverb has it, *noblesse oblige*, and our nobility now obliges us to add to this antecedent the greater triumph of a complete and heartfelt reconciliation, Civil war, everywhere and always, proverbial for the inveteracy of its venom, often passing from generation to generation with the blood, shall here become a savor of life unto life, not of death unto death. By the blessing of God and the magnanimity of the people, its baleful fires shall not smoulder in their ashes, but be extinguished by their ashes. By the blessing of God and the magnamity of the people, this centennial year, this hundredth birthday of the time which saw the self-sacrifice and devotion of the fathers shall seal the bond of an indissoluble unity among the children. It shall be a year not of enmity and alienation, but of sweet renewals and generous affections. The genius of harmony shall inspire it, and a loving concord shall bless it! Amen! Amen! and again I say, Amen! From the dark mounds where our common parents lie buried, come ten thousand hallowed voices which cry to us, Amen! In the future, too, I see the form of the Republic, still young and beautiful and strong, and I hear the immortal music of her lips as they send back, Amen! Let every American heart, then, repeat the solemn adjuration, till it fills every valley and echoes from every hill-top, and rises like a majestic anthem of the people. to meet the responses of the choiring Heavens: Amen!

www.ingramcontent.com/pod-product-compliance
Lightning Source LLC
LaVergne TN
LVHW011134110826
845150LV00008B/2336
* 9 7 8 1 4 1 8 1 9 4 1 3 0 *